BIJOU LE TORD

A Bird or Two

A Story about Henri Matisse

EERDMANS BOOKS FOR YOUNG READERS

GRAND RAPIDS, MICHIGAN   CAMBRIDGE, U. K.

For Yannickou and Kiku
with love.

Text and illustrations
Copyright © 1999 by Bijou LeTord
Published 1999 by Eerdmans Books for Young Readers
An imprint of Wm. B. Eerdmans Publishing Company
255 Jefferson S.E., Grand Rapids, Michigan 49503
P.O. Box 163, Cambridge CB3 9PU U.K.

Printed in the United States of America

04   7 6 5 4 3

Library of Congress Cataloging-in-Publication Data

Le Tord, Bijou.
A bird or two: a story about Henri Matisse / written and illustrated by Bijou Le Tord.
p.   cm.
Summary: Simple text and bright illustrations describe the work of French painter, Henri Matisse, particularly his joyful use of color.
ISBN 0-8028-5184-3   (hardcover)
Matisse, Henri, 1869–1954—Themes, motives—Juvenile literature.
Color in art—Juvenile literature.
[1. Matisse, Henri, 1869–1954. 2. Artists. 3. Painting, French. 4. Art appreciation.] I. Title.
ND553.M37L34   1999
759.4—dc21   98-55108
CIP
AC

The text type was set in Gill Sans.
The book was designed by Willem Mineur.

Author's Note

Henri Matisse made many trips to Nice (pronounced *Neece* in French) while he lived and painted in Paris. Later in his life he decided to move there permanently. By then he already was an accomplished artist, painter, and sculptor. He also knew colors better than almost anyone. Matisse felt immensely fortunate to have found Nice, a place of such luminosity and beauty.

After visiting Nice myself and discovering Matisse's environment, I decided to concentrate on the work he did while there. I also have represented one of his paintings of dancers from an earlier period of his work because it felt important to the story of the book and depicts a major period of Matisse's work.

Matisse felt that his colored paper cutouts were his best work. They reminded him of the beautiful light and colors that had intrigued him while he visited the Island of Tahiti. He "sculpted" — as he used to say — his paper cutouts using great big scissors. Matisse began this work in his early eighties when he was ill and no longer able to walk easily or sit at his easel. Matisse never gave up his work; he loved it until the end of his life.

It was my father who introduced me to Henri Matisse and who first taught me how to love Matisse's art — his drawings, sculptures, lithographs, and extraordinary paintings. My father was an artist who, like Matisse, was inspired by the richness and clarity of light in the South of France where we lived. When I was a child my first "picture books" were the beautiful volumes of Matisse's paintings in my father's library. For me, Matisse was as familiar and as close as a member of our family, and his work is forever tied to my memories of childhood. I have kept within me those images of France — its light, its colors, its great beauty. They have inspired me to create this book as a celebration of Henri Matisse and his magnificent work.

This is a partial list of museums where you can see Henri Matisse's paintings, drawings, paper cutouts, and sculptures:

FRANCE — GRENOBLE: Musée de Peintures et de Sculptures. PARIS: Le Musée D' Art Moderne, Centre Georges Pompidou; Le Musée de L'Orangerie; Le Musée Picasso. NICE: Le Musée Matisse (There you can see his favorite and famous "Rococo" or Venetian chair and other furnishings from his apartment/studio at the Hotel Regina where he lived.) VENCE: La Chapelle de Vence.
CANADA — OTTAWA: The National Gallery of Canada.
SWEDEN — STOCKHOLM: Moderna Museet.

RUSSIA — ST. PETERSBURG: The Hermitage Museum. MOSCOW: The Pushkin Museum of Fine Arts.
USA — NEW YORK: The Museum of Modern Art; The Metropolitan Museum. CHICAGO: The Art Institute of Chicago. BALTIMORE: The Baltimore Museum of Art: the Cone Collection. WASHINGTON DC: The National Gallery of Art. MERION: The Barnes Foundation. PITTSBURGH: The Carnegie Museum of Art. SAN FRANCISCO: The Museum of Modern Art.

When
Henri Matisse
returned
to Nice
in winter,
the brilliant sun
warmed
everything.
He looked
at the sea,
the palm trees,
and the sun
as if for
the first
time.

Because
of the
delicate
and
bright sun
of Nice,
Matisse's
colors
changed.

To his
color
palette
he
added
the bluest
sapphire
blue
he could
imagine.
And
with it
he
painted
the
Mediterranean
Sea.

Matisse thought, "I like it here. It is a paradise. I will paint greens greener than apples, yellows more yellow than lemons."

His friends
said,
"He paints
the sunshine
everyday.
He draws
everywhere,
everyone,
all the time.
He works
joyfully,
with a light
heart.
He is
enchanted."

There
were no
colors
Matisse
didn't like.
He loved
black and
painted it
just as he
would
any other
color.

He used it
on pure
white
paper
as a fine,
simple,
curving
line,
which he
called
an
arabesque.

He also
painted
it to show
the cool,
shady places
inside his
house
and
the light
filtering
from
the sun
outside.

Matisse
was so
delighted
with his new work
that he kept on
painting —
simply,
effortlessly.
All
his life
was in
harmony
with the way
he felt.
He wrote
to his friend
Bonnard,
also a painter,
"Long
live
painting!"

Matisse
could paint
the light
on a leaf
or the
slow-moving
branches
of palm trees
and
silvery
olive trees.

With
just
as much
ease,
he
could
paint
dancers
in
a round
dance

or joyful
ladies
in feathered hats
and pearls.

He also
sculpted
figures
in clay.
They too
were
cheerful
and filled
with love.

Matisse
made us
"hear"
with our
eyes
the music
he painted
in his
pictures.

He said,
"I am
strong
because
I do
what is
in my
mind."

Matisse
was
also
delicate
and
fragile.

He was
as beautiful
and
simple
as his paintings
of
mimosa flowers,
shells,
coral fish,
the sunshine,
and
a bird
or
two.